◆

DIANDRA WILLIAMS
MATTERS OF HEALING

AFFIRMATIONS AND JOURNAL

"Diandra Williams: Matters of Healing" is based on a true story. Some names and identifying details have been changed to protect the privacy of individuals.

Although the author and publisher have made every effort to ensure that the information in this book was correct at press time, the author and publisher do not assume and hereby disclaim any liability to any party for any loss, damage, or disruption caused by errors or omissions, whether such errors or omissions result from negligence, accident, or any other cause.

This book is not intended as a substitute for the medical advice of physicians. The reader should consult a physician in matters relating to her health and particularly with respect to any symptoms that may require diagnosis or medical attention.

Copyright © 2023 by Diandra Williams

All rights reserved. No part of this book may be reproduced or used in any manner without written permission of the author except for the use of quotations in a book review.

For more information, address: diandraw50@gmail.com

www.tfieldinglowecompany.com

Table of Contents

My Story..7

Affirmations/Journal Prompting...26

       Healing Is A Part Of God's Plan For My Life! ....

       Body Affirmations ....

       Mind Affirmations ....

       Finances Affirmation ....

Blank Journal Pages...89

About the Author..

CHILDHOOD

I was born to my parents, Helen Brown and Robert Chase, on December 2, 1979. My mom raised me with my brother Montel, who was five years older than me. When my mom was twenty-two, she was a single parent with two children and had only a high school education living in the south side of Providence, Rhode Island.

Providence was home to 179,000 people, of which 84.2% were citizens. As of 2020, 30.3% of Providence residents were born outside the country. In 2020, there were 1.75 times more White (Non-Hispanic) residents in Providence than any other race or ethnicity. There were 34.7k White (Hispanic) and 28.7k Other (Hispanic) residents, the second and third most common ethnic groups. In the early 90s, the city's south side was a melting pot of different cultures and people. I remember that the city was primarily Spanish and Black people, along with some Asian people. No matter the background, the neighborhood was built up of hard-working people.

My mom worked as a certified nursing assistant. While she was working her 7:00 a.m. to 3:00 p.m. shift, I attended Stewart Elementary School. Mom worked tirelessly to provide for us and meet all our needs. Even with that, times were hard, and while sometimes there was a lack of food, there was no lack of love. When I entered sixth grade at Roger Williams Middle School, I was lucky to find some friends who looked and sounded like me. We understood each other's home situations.

It wasn't until I entered high school that I understood how much we struggled financially—this moment of enlightenment in the 10th grade helped me become closer to my friend group, forming a strong bond. They were going through the same issues I experienced; lack of food in the refrigerator, utilities being shut off, and not having enough money to pay the rent.

Also, 10th grade was when I realized I needed my dad more in my life. I felt a massive void due to our infrequent visits. I no longer wanted to be the little girl that saw her dad periodically, but I needed to be a person with a stable relationship with her father. The fact that my mom was a victim of domestic violence with a man who was not my father

,was challenging, but I always wanted to be rescued by my dad from the horrific life I lived at home.

I took refuge in after-school activities and hung out with my best friend Jasmine and some boys. Being tall and thin with short hair - which was not the style in middle school then - it was amazing to get a compliment from a boy. I didn't have the confidence, I didn't feel beautiful, I didn't see people on TV that looked like me, and I rarely saw images in magazines. The occasional chance when I looked at an Ebony or Essence magazine while in a waiting room at the Welfare Office was maybe the one time I would get to see somebody who looked like me on the cover. In real life, I never did see a woman radiate such beauty and splendor in my neighborhood.

Later in high school, I found comfort in the arms of my first boyfriend, Keith, who would become my first son, Raekwon's father. Keith and I met in the 11th grade on a field trip to the White Mountains. He and I talked, laughed, and cracked on each other the entire bus ride. We decided to become boyfriend and girlfriend. Once again, trauma bonding over the fact that we were just trying to make it every day in high school, trying to be the cool kids, and trying to lie low of the wicked storm brewing and waiting for each of us at our homes. We were lucky we had each other for comfort through the hard times.

Shortly after our field trip to the White Mountains, I discovered I was pregnant. We weren't prepared to have a baby in our senior year of high school. That year was stressful and traumatizing; being young and pregnant, balancing homework and doctor's appointments, and trying to figure out if I could go to college on top of the daily struggle of living in a violent house.

My mom's boyfriend, Davon, was living with us. Davon was 5'11, 250 lbs, light skin with a caramel complexion, Billy D. Williams softly curled hair, and was gifted in music. He could sing and arrange music. Davon was a handsome devil in disguise. Most of my days in school were spent worrying about if my mom was getting beat up at home. I always thought I would one day walk into the house after school and find her dead.

Davon was not only abusive but also on crack. Having him in the house was a living hell. There were days when I came home to find her crying because they had been arguing. I never understood why she stayed so long in an unhappy relationship. Once, she told me when Davon asked her out on her first date, she heard God say "No," but when she opened her mouth, she said "Yes." God telling her "No" was a warning that she would suffer through the twelve years of domestic violence.

The worst days were when she greeted my brother and me at the front door, saying, "Hi, how was school?" and "watch your step." This meant they had been physically fighting, and she was now cleaning up the aftermath. Lamps, drinking glasses, plates, and phones were strewn about the apartment and broken to pieces - remnants of my mom's attempts to defend herself against Davon's attack.

One day, my mom had finally had enough. I came home from school greeted by my grandmother sitting on the sofa. I instinctively knew something was wrong. I thought my worst feeling had come true- that my mom had not survived a fight with Davon. My grandmother told me my mom had been attacked again by her abuser, but this time, it was a near-fatal stabbing for Davon. I was shocked. I could not believe it, so I entered her room to see if she was waiting for me.

As I looked around the room, I saw the wood soaked in blood, and I knew that my grandmother was telling the truth. Later, I discovered how things could have turned out for my mom. Luckily for her, the abuse was documented every time the police were called to our home over the ten years of their relationship. The evidence saved my mother's life and changed our lives as a family. The justice system finally came to her aid and gave her a way out to live a better life. My mom never looked back but looked forward and rebuilt her life from the ground up. Only God's hand kept us alive to live through this dark period to tell the story.

MOTHERHOOD, MARRIAGE & MINISTRY

During the spring of my senior year, three significant events happened. April 21st, 1999, I had my son at 19 years old. In May of that year, I went to senior prom, and then in June, I graduated from high school. A single parent fresh out of high school, I chose to stay with my mom for the first two years of Raekwon's life. I was nowhere near prepared to raise a child alone because I was still basically a child and struggling to find a way to support us on my own. I decided to go to cosmetology school in addition to applying for United University Heights affordable housing.

In December of 2000, I was approved for housing at University Heights. I remember the joy I felt. After a year and a half of living with Mom, I could finally move out and be on my own with my baby boy. My beginnings of being independent were humble. I had a futon, his baby bed, my bed, and a kitchen table set that cost me $129. I borrowed a television and TV stand, and we moved in that weekend. While we didn't have much starting, I had my baby, and that was all that mattered to me.

That first year, Raekwon's dad, Keith, would stop by occasionally to visit his son and to drop off child support money. During one of those visits, I asked Keith if he would like to get back together and move into the apartment. He said no to both questions. My heart was broken, but I knew he wasn't as prepared as I was for being a young parent. My dream was for us to rekindle the high school flame we started and be grown-up parents to Raekwon. In my mind, I believed we could work together and build something great. I wanted my son to have two parents, which was more than I grew up with. For me, a two-parent home meant stability, even if there was not enough money all the time. God had other plans.

I learned to raise Raekwon the best I could by bringing him up in church - the church my Aunt Patrice brought me to when I was seven. It was a small Pentecostal church on on Ocean Street on the south side of

Providence. I grew spiritually under Bishop Elizabeth Scurry's and the late Pastor Allen Harrison's leadership.

Growing up, hearing my mother pray at home intrigued me. Who was this God she always cried out to in prayer? While running errands on the weekends, Mom would have a stack of small Bible tracks in her pocketbook. Wherever she was, when she felt led by the Holy Spirit to offer the prayer of salvation, she would stop what she was doing and minister to them. She would go into prayer with that person on the spot. Many received salvation through the work my mother continues to do. I received the call and anointing through her as an intercessory prayer warrior.

Faith in Action Ministries was a Bible-based, family-run, and family-oriented church. I was very active in their church. I was busy attending school and church on Wednesdays, Sundays, and the occasional Friday, the first couple of years of being alone. The church became a place I brought my burdens about being a teenage mother and having a baby out of wedlock. Raising Raekwon alone, I became depressed and scared because, as much as I was happy being independent, I had no clue what I was doing, and I was doing it alone. Church saved my life. I constantly worried about how a Black woman would raise a Black boy to be a Black man. Even though I was scared, I spent those first years alone with Raekwon focusing on us and building our home.

In 2003, I met my husband, Jason, through the church. It was during an outreach service led by Pastor Allen Harrison at the Rhode Island Training School, a facility meant to rehabilitate juvenile delinquents. When we first met during that church service, neither of us would have predicted we would be dating each other in the near future. As a Faith in Action Ministries member, the congregation and myself witnessed on Sundays or Wednesday bible study that young men recently released from the Training School popping in to speak with Pastor Harrison. The young men were sometimes bashful and ashamed of their testimony. One thing was evident - every time each young man

wandered into the church, they intentionally expressed how much of an impact Pastor Harrison and his Ministry had on their life at the Training School. Pastor Harrison would always say, "Keep a song in your heart, a simple song to help keep you focused and to worship the Lord in season and out of season."

Jason visited the Faith in Action Ministries almost a year after we attended the Training School ministry. I could see he was one of those young men returning from the Training School with a testimony. Pastor Harrison took him under his wing to work closely on odd jobs around the church and its grounds.

Pastor Harrison was a big strong manly man with a smile that lit up and filled the room with a radiating breath of love. He was a big old teddy bear with a heart to help his community. His life is remembered by the works and testimony of the many young men and women he helped.

In 2003, Pastor Harrison spent countless hours working on the church bus. Keeping the bus serviced and prepared was a passion for him. He used that time with Jason to teach him basic mechanics skills and life lessons he knew a young man needed. Pastor Harrison saw Jason had nothing but free time on his hands and a willing spirit to help out. I believe God placed Pastor Harrison in Jason's life to be a father figure.

Right away, I saw there was something different about Jason. I was never attracted to anyone who attended or visited the church, but he became the exception. He was 5'10 and had big muscles, beautiful, almost glowing ocean blue eyes, and a great smile. He wasn't automatically my type because he was White. I was not prejudiced but more curious about his type because I was a young African American female with a three-year-old son. Nevertheless, Jason's good-looking physical appearance, his growth under the wing of Pastor Harrison, and what seemed like his never-ending presence at the church made him more appealing each time I saw him. While crossing paths exiting the church building, he casually spoke to me one day. I was shocked that he even noticed me. We talked briefly, and weeks later, I found out he asked Pastor Harrison about me

and my situation with my son. All there was to know was that I was a single mom raising my son with the Lord's help and the church's help. Surprisingly, that didn't scare Jason away from talking to me again. He approached me smoothly and casually, asked for my phone number. This was back when we exchanged phone numbers and not social media QR codes.

When Jason wasn't with Pastor Harrison, he was at home with his mother and stepdad, usually talking on the phone with me. We started at the basics, discussing each other's favorite colors, foods, and things to do. As the days and weeks passed, our conversations became more intense. I was curious about what he saw and wanted from me. As a single mom, I was cautious. At the time, I was still living in an apartment in University Heights and was working part-time. I considered returning to school, trying to find a career that could provide a financially comfortable life for my son and me. Looking back, I didn't feel like the ideal candidate to date a single, handsome, 20-something-year-old man with no children and his whole life ahead of him.

Jason assured me he was fine dating someone with a young child. We agreed to continue getting to know each other through phone conversations. We even exchanged little love notes like kids used to do back in the day during class. We were corny according to today's online dating standards, but it was exciting and fun at the time. We tried to talk as much as we could, adding up to several dates and countless hours on the phone. Sometimes it was a struggle to go out or talk on the phone as our schedules were so busy- we couldn't talk or go out on a Wednesday

because it was Bible study night or a Friday cause that was prayer night at the church. It couldn't be a Tuesday either because that was when we did outreach church service at the Training School. Also, I was a full-time student at Newport School of Hairdressing in Pawtucket, RI. To support my son and myself, I took the skills I learned at cosmetology school and opened a small beauty shop out of my house. I did hair right out of my kitchen with many clients from my local churches. Women often came to get their hair done on a Friday to be ready for Sunday service. Their support helped me pay the bills.

When I finished school, my clients in my kitchen followed me to my first job in a salon, where I worked for seven years. Somehow we made it work, and we navigated our way through dating. Our feelings grew for each other, and I was ready to see what the next level was for us.

Jason and I would use notebooks to write our notes to one another, and one day I told him that I felt God was telling me he was supposed to be my husband. He asked what that meant, so I explained that I felt strongly in my heart and spirit. God wanted us to get to know each other, to date exclusively to get married intentionally. I explained God's plan for the family found in Genesis 1 and several other scripture passages. Jason understood where I was coming from.

Looking back, I can see that I was right - God did want us to be married. However, it wasn't supposed to be as quickly as we thought, as we were not equipped to be married at such a young age. The Lord led Pastor Harrison to sit down with us individually to see what we were thinking regarding our relationship. After only six months of dating, we wanted to get married. Jason was still living with his mother and stepfather with no job, only helping out the Pastor at the church several days a week. On the other hand, I lived in my own apartment with my now four-year-old son. Pastor Harrison, as a spiritual father, strongly advised us, both separately and in a conversation with the three of us, not to get married so soon. He said we were too young and inexperienced in the world. Jason was not prepared financially to help support Raekwon and me. Most importantly, he was in no way prepared to instantly become a father to a child that was not his.

Everything the Pastor said made sense, but I didn't understand why we couldn't get married and figure things out. I was disappointed because I wanted to hear, "Yes, marry this guy. He's a good guy." Pastor Harrison's godson, Bishop Michael Stokes Jr., advised us not to marry so soon. Bishop Stokes knew what he was talking about because he and his wife, Ruth, were married at 16 years old in high school when Ruth was pregnant.

At the time, I was angry at the Pastor because I thought he would be supportive like a dad and tell us what we wanted to hear. Now I understand he was being a supportive dad by telling us what we needed to hear. He was telling us these things to protect me from hardship and struggle. Also, he was protecting Jason because he wasn't prepared for the level of responsibility I had already assumed - paying bills, working, and caring for a child. Jason would be new to being a step-parent, and he would be expected to help support what I had already built for my son Raekwon.

Jason and I heard what everyone had to say about not getting married, but we didn't listen. Twenty years later, I can see how God tried to warn me. Amid this, on April 28th, 2001, my big brother Montel Williams was murdered by a friend outside of a nightclub in Providence. Montel's sudden death destroyed me emotionally and mentally. The graphic nature of the incident was too much to bear, on top of going to the hospital in the wee hours of the morning with my mother to identify my brother's body. It was too much for anyone. I was unprepared to see him lying on the ambulance stretcher inside the trauma room with tubes in his nose and blood on his shirt where the bullets had entered his shoulder and heart.

Pastor Harrison was always in my life to encourage and support me when I needed him and the church family. They supported my family and me through the entire ordeal of my brother's wake, funeral, and the trial and conviction of the man who murdered my brother, Wayne. Shortly after my brother's death, I went through a period where I experienced suicidal thoughts. I was preoccupied with the idea of suicide. It clouded my mind, and I felt desperate for the peace it would bring. I felt helpless, abandoned, and unprotected. All of the struggles of my past became burdens I couldn't shoulder- not having my father in my life, my son's father leaving us, and my brother's death. I felt I had no reason to live and was ready to die.

One night after church, I prepared myself to drive my blue Thunderbird into a tree on

15

the corner of my street. I planned to leave Raekwon strapped into his car seat, remove it from the car, and leave him out of harm's way across the street. Once I did that, I would throw my car in reverse and drive into the tree as fast as possible. Before I could even get my hands to unbuckle my seatbelt, I heard the Holy Spirit say, "What about your son?"

Tears began to stream down my face. Shame, guilt, and grief came over me like a heavy winter coat I couldn't take off. The tears wouldn't stop flowing. I asked God to forgive me for wanting to take the life He gave me and for wanting to abandon my son. The Holy Spirit spoke to me out of love and concern. God extended Raekwon and me grace and mercy that night.

I had thought I had conquered my demons in the years as a single parent before meeting Jason. Regaining control of my emotional and mental health had been an uphill battle. When Jason and I met, I thought my emotions and mental health were in a place of stability. Suicidal thoughts - thoughts Jason knew nothing about - were behind me in the past. The people that did know the trauma I had faced were the same people telling me not to get married. They knew the ugly details of how Satan came to kill, steal, and destroy people, including my mind and my will to live. They knew I wasn't ready.

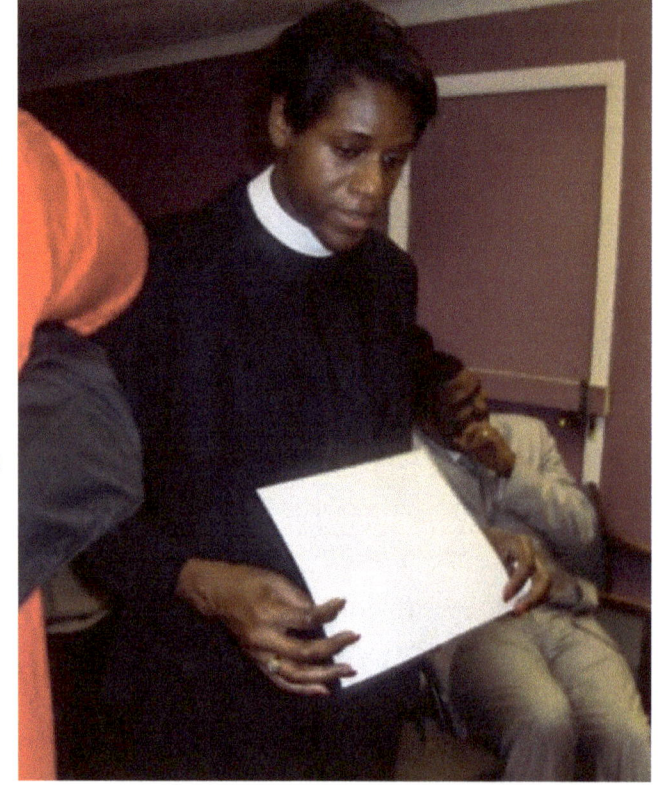

Pastor Harrison was the voice of reason for me during this time, but being young and strong-willed, we still wanted to be married. I wanted to build a family of my own to heal the pain of my broken family. I wanted Jason to be a father to Raekwon, a role that his biological father refused to take. I wanted to be chosen and protected by a man who wanted to share a life with me. It didn't matter that he didn't have money, a car, or anything to offer but himself. I had all those things and was making enough money to support myself and my son. Being a man who loved me with potential was enough for me to want to marry Jason.

Against all the advice, Jason and I were married on New Year's Eve 2002, a few hours before midnight, in my University Heights apartment. Our marriage started with Jason moving into my two-bedroom apartment, again with humble beginnings of a small home and little money. With our few material resources, we made it work for our home.

Shortly after, we suffered a miscarriage. It was a devastating loss, and I thought God was punishing me for something I had done in my past. This brought on depression. At a follow-up doctor's visit, the doctor explained that I had done nothing past or present and that sometimes the body naturally aborts a pregnancy for no known reason. Knowing this information helped Jason and me to understand what happened to our beloved baby. On December 17th, 2003, almost a year after we were married, we had our rainbow baby Takesha. She was 9 lbs. 10 oz.

As a couple, we thought our family was complete with two children, Raekwon and Takesha, but we were in for another surprise! On September 9th, 2005, I gave birth to our son Montel Jordan: another miracle and a very large baby at 9 lbs. and 11 oz. The stress of trying to deliver Montel put him and me in danger. I went into cardiac arrest, and my mom was given the choice to save the baby or me. I told my mom to choose the life of my son Montel. He was named after my deceased brother, and his middle name Jordan was a transitional place of cleansing. Luckily they were able to save us both.

That year became one of many transitions for me. One month after giving birth, I transitioned to a new ministry, Word of Truth, under the leadership of then Bishop Michael Stokes Jr and his wife. Already an ordained minister at my previous church under the leadership of Pastor Harrison, I resumed that position at my new ministry. Jason remained under the leadership of Pastor Harrison for a few months. Being in two different churches was a strain on our marriage.

We were already working different schedules as I was a cosmetologist working full days from Tuesday to Saturday. Jason worked at a local event center as a runner and customer service rep. His work hours would clash with my schedule so much we didn't see each other until it was time for me to pick him up at work. The kids would be sleeping by the time we settled down at home. We were two people living together but passing each other as we went through life.

Married life wasn't playing out as I had envisioned. My prayers to God were to make us a happy, united family. Prayer has been the one constant thing in my life since the age of twelve years old. If it had not been for prayer, I wouldn't have known how to handle my struggling marriage. My husband and I were trying to define our roles as parents, partners, lovers, and ministers. This search kept us at the feet of Christ Jesus, looking for direction. We also were off and on in counseling as a couple and separately with our Bishop Michael Stokes. Working on our marriage through counseling and prayer strengthened the anointing in my life. The level of dedication to devotional time with the Lord added value to my ministry.

Bishop Stokes saw the growth evident in my life. Ordained as an elder, I was the lead elder over the intercessory prayer team. Under my leadership, we met twice a week for prayer. Diligently, I was working with the members helping to plant the seed of prayer in our weekly meeting. The seed grew into people educated about prayer with the knowledge of how to activate it with power every time they prayed. The intercessory prayer team I led would take me to the next dimension in kingdom work as an ordained Pastor.

My husband and I served together as a team - a powerful team destroying the works of the kingdom of Satan. My husband's testimony and work ethic serving as an adjutant and elder was evidence that he had more work to do. Bishop Stokes saw the next step for us as a couple in ministry, and we became ordained as Pastors. Our call was to expand the local footprint of the headquarters church and branch out into our local church. Our first church was a storefront located on Charles Street in Providence.

Unfortunately, I faced unexpected health issues, and we had to close our little church. Bishop Stokes advised us to return home to headquarters church until things cleared up with my health. I was very vocal about not wanting to return to the headquarters church. I felt like a failure. In my mind, I was comparing this return to our spiritual home to a young adult who leaves home for the first time only to return home to their parent's house because they weren't prepared for the real world. The real world wasn't what I expected. Realistically neither my Bishop, my husband, nor myself was prepared in any fashion as to what God was about to do as we returned to our spiritual home. God knew what I needed in the long run.

direction. We also were off and on in counseling both together as a couple and separately with our Bishop Michael Stokes. Working on our marriage through counseling and prayer strengthened the anointing in my life. The level of dedication to devotional time with the Lord added value to my ministry.

Bishop Stokes saw the growth evident in my life. Ordained as an elder, I was the lead elder over the intercessory prayer team. Under my leadership, we met twice a week for prayer. Diligently, I was working with the members helping to plant the seed of prayer in our weekly meeting. The seed grew into people educated about prayer with the knowledge of how to activate it with power every time they prayed. The intercessory prayer team I lead would take me to the next dimension in Kingdom work as an ordained Pastor.

My husband and I served together as a team - a powerful team destroying the works of the kingdom of Satan. My husband's testimony and work ethic serving as an adjutant and elder was evidence that he had more work to do. Bishop Stokes saw the next step for us as a couple in ministry, and we became ordained as Pastors. Our call was to expand the local footprint of the headquarters church and branch out into our own local church. Our first church was a storefront located on Charles Street in Providence.

Unfortunately, I faced some unexpected health issues, and we had to close our little church. Bishop Stokes advised us to return home to headquarters church until things cleared up with my health. I was very vocal about not wanting to return to the headquarters church. I felt like a failure. In my mind, I was comparing this return back to our spiritual home to a young adult that leaves home for the first time only to return back home to their parent's house because they weren't prepared for the real world. The real world wasn't what I expected. Realistically neither my Bishop, my husband, nor myself was prepared in any fashion as to what God was about to do as we returned to our spiritual home. God knew what I needed in the long run.

EVERYDAY

Married life was sometimes very predictable, considering much of our free time was spent in church. Our children went to the local public schools and participated in community activities sponsored by the community centers. When they weren't at the community center playing with the neighborhood kids, we were at Bible study, church-sponsored field trips, and anything else centered around our church family.

As a family, the outside world was not something we purposely mixed with. We were so involved with the church that our money was usually spent on offerings and sowing seeds to fortify the Kingdom of God. Our pockets often filled the gap to ensure our leaders and church had what they needed.

Our money was not spent on ourselves but on helping a greater cause. Even though our everyday life centered around the church, we didn't envy those families who went to theme parks and took big vacations. We were so heavily engulfed in church life we only saw our extended families periodically on different occasions.

We didn't consciously try to be involved in worldly deeds. We were taught that the Kingdom of God is more important than the Kingdom of man. Not seeing our family was unknowingly putting strain on our marriage, as we were solely dedicated to living by the Word and did not care what the world had to say.

ILLNESS

The afternoon of February 6th, 2013, started like any other day. When I woke that morning, I had no clue that something would happen- the beginning of the end of the world I knew. The threads of my life would unravel as something deep within me came to the surface, something no one would know how to fix. It destroyed my body, my mind, and ultimately my marriage. February 6th was the Big Bang that changed my life and me forever.

My kids came home from school, and I was napping before I had to get up and prepare for work. At the time, I worked 4 pm-12 am as direct support staff in a group home for women coming off drugs and alcohol. As I woke from my afternoon nap, I felt this odd heavy sensation in my legs. I tried to swing them around to the front of the bed, but I could not move them. My lower extremities had fallen asleep; no matter what I did, I could not wake them up. I went to move my hand to brace myself to get up off the bed, but I couldn't feel my fingers. I tried to grip the sheets. I yelled to my husband, "My hands aren't working! My hands aren't working!" He yelled from the kitchen, "What do you mean your hands are not working?"

I was hysterically crying. In my mind, I was trying to figure out why my legs felt like cinder blocks and were tingling, in addition to understanding why my hands were not functioning. My husband entered the room, trying to console me and figure out what was happening. I couldn't move. The pain was unbearable, and I felt like my body was frozen. My arms, legs, fingers, and toes were stuck in place with an odd numbing sensation. And did I mention the extreme pain I was feeling?

I felt like a soda can that someone had stepped on, crushing me. My husband picked me up, carried me to the car, and rushed me to Miriam Hospital. I don't remember filling out paperwork or sitting down. I remember being on a gurney with doctors over me, questioning why I was crying, yelling, and making a scene. My husband tried to explain that I woke up like this, unable to get out of bed.

The doctors asked many questions, some very embarrassing, like did I use drugs? My answer was no. I felt that they thought maybe I was drug-seeking, not really in pain but looking for a fix of narcotics. They asked me if I could have been drugged by someone else. Then, they asked my husband to step out, and the questions became more offensive. The doctor asked if my husband was abusing me, if I thought he had he had poisoned me, and if I felt safe at home. They wanted to know if our relationship was ok and if I had any other sexual partners. The answer to those questions was just plain and simple, no. I felt safe; I wasn't being poisoned. I was committed to my marriage and husband faithfully and in every possible way. As bizarre as these questions were, I later understood they asked for my safety. At the time, I was in so much pain I just wanted them to find a solution to what was wrong with me.

After the questions, they drew blood and filled nine vials to test for everything from HIV, AIDS, STDS, and Lyme Disease to rare viruses. After hours of waiting, doctors returned to tell me they thought I had a rare virus causing my inflammation markers to be so high as well as driving my joints to swell up and be in pain. The emergency room doctor diagnosed me with cellulitis, a potentially serious bacterial skin infection. The affected skin is typically swollen, sometimes painful, and warm to the touch. Cellulitis usually affects the lower legs but can occur on the face, arms, and other body areas. The ER doctor sent me home with prednisolone and extra strength ibuprofen. I spent four months going through extreme inflammation, specifically swelling in my knees, ankles, and elbows, and having fevers and bruising on my face.

It took me four and a half months to find the proper doctor to diagnose my illness. My search landed me at Eastside Rheumatology in Pawtucket, Rhode Island, under the care of Dr. Camilla Hunt. On my first visit, she asked me for my story. We discussed my history as a mom, wife, and working pastor. Dr. Hunt wanted us to figure out what brought on this sudden attack of inflammation throughout my body, as my lifestyle was not an indicator of something inwardly wrong.

It was clear to Dr. Hunt and anyone else who saw me in person that something was happening with my body. I had gained 50 lbs in four months from the medication I was prescribed - the prednisone, other steroids, and narcotics were not keeping the inflammation and pain at bay, but they were causing side effects. After several months of tests and visits, Dr. Hunt finally diagnosed me with rheumatoid arthritis in January 2014. Being officially diagnosed with rheumatoid arthritis (RA) was the breakthrough I needed in my prayers. I desperately wanted to know for a year what was wrong with me, what had happened, and why we couldn't find an answer. Being diagnosed was validating; I could point to a cause for all of the sufferings I had been through.

Dr. Hunt warned me that autoimmune diseases like RA usually come in pairs if not multiples. Rheumatoid arthritis was the answer to why my fingers, wrists, and ankles were swollen and highly inflamed, but it didn't explain other symptoms I was having. I was experiencing a burning sensation on my back that would not go away, sensitivity to touch, and muscle weakness in my legs and hips. Sometimes I would also experience muscle weakness in my hands that would cause me to drop objects. These weren't the systems of rheumatoid arthritis. Dr. Hunt advised me to keep a health journal of the symptoms I was experiencing. This was a way to create a timeline of events that may have triggered the symptoms. Every time I would have pain, I would jot down the date, the time, how I felt physically and emotionally, and what I was doing when the pain started.

After about six weeks of journaling every detail about the pain, I began experiencing sudden fatigue that felt like I was sleepwalking. The sudden onset was unbearable. When the moment would wash over me if I didn't lie down, my body would start to slow down, my eyes would get heavy so that I could barely keep them open, my breathing would be labored, and it felt like I was going to pass out and never wake up. My muscles were so weak there would be days I would get up from lying down just to fall on the floor.

One day my husband came out of the living room, and as he turned his head to go into the kitchen, he found me crawling on my hands and knees out of the bedroom, trying to make it to the bathroom before I urinated on myself. He picked me up off the floor, carried me to the bathroom, and put me on the toilet. My body had humiliated me in front of my husband. I needed more answers.

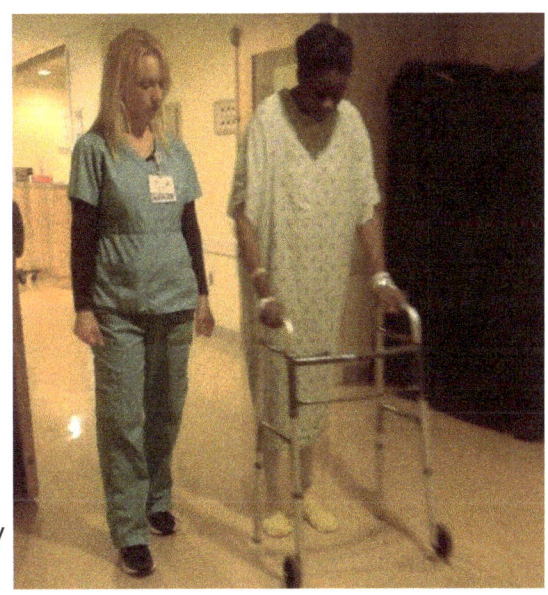

There were many times I questioned why God would do this to me. I was supposed to be enjoying my husband and children. I thought God was punishing me for a sin I committed in my teens. Also, I felt God would not allow the doctors to find out what was wrong with me because, in my mind, it was part of his punishment. Living trapped in a body of joints full of inflammation, a butterfly rash on my face, sore legs and fingers that worked only when they wanted to, and an overweight body I was uncomfortable in was physical torture. My depression returned.

Thankfully, God was not punishing me. Keeping a health journal and various testing helped Dr. Hunt come to a second diagnosis - that I had developed two new autoimmune diseases called fibromyalgia and dermatomyositis. Fibromyalgia is a disorder characterized by widespread musculoskeletal pain, fatigue, sleep, memory, and mood issues. Researchers believe that fibromyalgia amplifies painful sensations by affecting how your brain and spinal cord process painful and non-painful signals. Fibromyalgia often coexists with conditions such as irritable bowel syndrome, chronic fatigue syndrome, migraines, interstitial cystitis or painful bladder syndrome, temporomandibular joint disorders, anxiety, depression, and postural tachycardia syndrome. With dermatomyositis, sufferers can experience pain in the muscles and joints, various skin symptoms such as redness, darkening, and patches of thick dry skin, muscle weakness, fatigue, difficulty swallowing, multiple-joint inflammation, pneumonia from inhaling oral secretions, puffy eyes, or weight loss.

2014 ended with my triple diagnosis from Dr. Hunt, with plenty of medication to reduce inflammation, pain, and swelling. In 2015, life took another turn for the worse. The medication I was taking to reduce the inflammation and pain caused both hip joints to deteriorate. I developed avascular necrosis in both hips and to compound it all, I became pregnant.

At 35, I was in my first trimester of pregnancy with our fourth child. It was truly a miracle as the medication I had taken for a year, a chemotherapy drug meant to help with the RA, had supposedly left me sterile. The avascular necrosis in both hip joints while pregnant made walking unbearable. I used a cane to get around. Each step felt like I was being kicked in my hip bones. Tears would stream down my cheeks. Pain medicine at that point didn't work because I was pregnant and couldn't be on high doses of narcotics. If I did take them, there was a high probability that the unborn baby would be born addicted to narcotics.

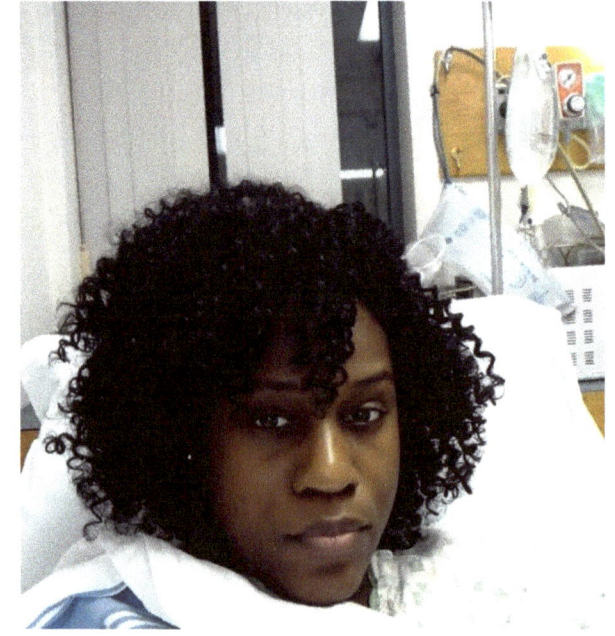

Our fourth baby, Danielle Nicole, was born on October 5th, 2015. In March of the following year, I had my first hip replacement, followed by three months of physical and occupational therapy. In July 2016, my other hip was replaced, followed by four months of physical and occupational therapy. By Danielle's first birthday, I could use my cane to take steady steps. I would often joke that Danielle and I learned to walk together.

Each year my health improved, and I was determined to come off heavy doses of steroids and pain medicine. Working hard to use all-natural food and portion control, I lost the weight I gained before my diagnosis. Reducing my weight and taking control of my diet helped to eliminate some of the medicines that I was taking. It was still a daily battle with fibromyalgia and rheumatoid arthritis, so my health issues did not end there.

In 2018, I developed fibroids and endometriosis, which resulted in a hysterectomy in April 2019. Also, I learned that I had Kein Box disease in my left wrist that same year. That led to yet another surgery in January 2020 for my wrist. I was due to return to work in April, but the COVID pandemic prevented me from completing my physical and occupational therapy.

Honestly, the pandemic was the best thing that could happen to me. I survived COVID twice while working on my emotional and mental health, allowing me to take my healing to the next level. Shelter in place prompted me to remember the good habits that helped me to heal my body previously - taking control of my food.

Purposeful living changed my life, and it did it again. I am in a better place mentally, emotionally, and physically because I challenged God to heal me on the level I wanted for years. Now I have experienced it. I have the calling to move forward and to show other women how they can heal physically, mentally, and emotionally to make their lives the abundant life Scripture calls us to live.

AFFIRMATIONS

HEALING IS PART OF GOD'S PLAN FOR MY LIFE!

"Pain Will Not Last Forever"

PERSONAL NOTE

Some days it felt like my arthritis pain took over my life. There will be day's on your health journey when the pain seems to be a dark cloud hovering over your life. It's important to remember pain is a temporary set back.

Let pain serve as a reminder to enjoy your good day with purpose.

SCRIPTURE

Heal me, O Lord, and I will be healed; save me and I will be saved, for you are the one I praise." ~ Jeremiah 17:14

Write a letter to your pain.

Mental Health Check-In

DATE _____

HOW ARE YOU FEELING TODAY? _____

HOW ARE YOU FEELING TODAY?

HOW CAN YOU IMPROVE YOUR MENTAL HEALTH? _____

WHAT HAVE BEEN YOUR THREE DOMINANT EMOTIONS THIS WEEK?
- _____
- _____
- _____

WHAT DO YOU FEEL GOOD ABOUT RIGHT NOW? _____

THINGS THAT TRIGGERS NEGATIVE EMOTIONS
- _____
- _____
- _____
- _____

MY RANKING OF MY MENTAL HEALTH THIS WEEK
☆ ☆ ☆ ☆ ☆

HEALING IS PART OF GOD'S PLAN FOR MY LIFE!

"Without a Diagnosis You Cannot be Healed"

PERSONAL NOTE

Don't be afraid of the diagnosis or the doctors. Without a diagnosis you cannot be healed. You do not know what to pray for.

SCRIPTURE

So do not fear, for I am with you; do not be dismayed, for I am your God. I will strengthen you and help you; I will uphold you with my righteous right hand." ~ Isaiah 41:10

How has your diagnosis changed your life for the better?

Mental Health Check-In

DATE _____

HOW ARE YOU FEELING TODAY?

HOW ARE YOU FEELING TODAY?

HOW CAN YOU IMPROVE YOUR MENTAL HEALTH?

WHAT HAVE BEEN YOUR THREE DOMINANT EMOTIONS THIS WEEK?
- _____
- _____
- _____

WHAT DO YOU FEEL GOOD ABOUT RIGHT NOW?

THINGS THAT TRIGGERS NEGATIVE EMOTIONS
- _____
- _____
- _____
- _____

MY RANKING OF MY MENTAL HEALTH THIS WEEK
☆ ☆ ☆ ☆ ☆

HEALING IS PART OF GOD'S PLAN FOR MY LIFE!

"What does Healing Look Like in the Future?"

PERSONAL NOTE

I thought being healed I would be back to my old self again. As my health yoyoed up and down I felt like I was dying on the inside. My personality changed. My views on life changed. What was once important seemed to no longer mean anything. I had to grieve losing the old me in order to be born again. Once I let go of the idea of ever being the old me again my health began to improve. My emotional health improved with it.

SCRIPTURE

"But I will restore you to health and heal your wounds,' declares the LORD" ~ Jeremiah 30:17

What are some fun and adventures you'd like to do once your health improve

Mental Health Check-In

DATE _____

HOW ARE YOU FEELING TODAY?

HOW ARE YOU FEELING TODAY?

HOW CAN YOU IMPROVE YOUR MENTAL HEALTH? _____

WHAT HAVE BEEN YOUR THREE DOMINANT EMOTIONS THIS WEEK?
- _____
- _____
- _____

WHAT DO YOU FEEL GOOD ABOUT RIGHT NOW? _____

THINGS THAT TRIGGERS NEGATIVE EMOTIONS
- _____
- _____
- _____
- _____

MY RANKING OF MY MENTAL HEALTH THIS WEEK

☆ ☆ ☆ ☆ ☆

HEALING IS PART OF GOD'S PLAN FOR MY LIFE!

"There is Purpose in the Process"

PERSONAL NOTE

Finding the purpose, the wisdom of going through a health crisis.

SCRIPTURE

You restored me to health and let me live. Surely it was for my benefit that I suffered such anguish. In your love you kept me from the pit of destruction; you have put all my sins behind your back." ~ Isaiah 38:16-17

Have you found your purpose through your health crisis?

Mental Health Check-In

DATE _____

HOW ARE YOU FEELING TODAY? _____

HOW ARE YOU FEELING TODAY? _____

HOW CAN YOU IMPROVE YOUR MENTAL HEALTH? _____

WHAT HAVE BEEN YOUR THREE DOMINANT EMOTIONS THIS WEEK?
- _____
- _____
- _____

WHAT DO YOU FEEL GOOD ABOUT RIGHT NOW? _____

THINGS THAT TRIGGERS NEGATIVE EMOTIONS
- _____
- _____
- _____
- _____

MY RANKING OF MY MENTAL HEALTH THIS WEEK
☆ ☆ ☆ ☆ ☆

BODY AFFIRMATIONS AND DECLARATIONS

I am worthy of rest.

PERSONAL NOTE

STOP and make yourself a priority and rest

SCRIPTURE

"By the seventh day God had finished the work he had been doing; so on the seventh day he rested from all his work. Then God blessed the seventh day and made it holy, because on it he rested from all the work of creating that he had done".
Genesis 2:2-3

What is stopping you from putting you first?

Mental Health Check-In

DATE _____

HOW ARE YOU FEELING TODAY? _____

HOW ARE YOU FEELING TODAY? _____

HOW CAN YOU IMPROVE YOUR MENTAL HEALTH? _____

WHAT HAVE BEEN YOUR THREE DOMINANT EMOTIONS THIS WEEK?
- _____
- _____
- _____

WHAT DO YOU FEEL GOOD ABOUT RIGHT NOW? _____

THINGS THAT TRIGGERS NEGATIVE EMOTIONS
- _____
- _____
- _____
- _____

MY RANKING OF MY MENTAL HEALTH THIS WEEK

☆ ☆ ☆ ☆ ☆

BODY AFFIRMATIONS AND DECLARATIONS

My Body Deserves Rest

PERSONAL NOTE

Your physical body can't keep going. Your body is prompting you to rest.

SCRIPTURE

In vain you rise early and stay up late, toiling for food to eat—for he grants sleep to those he loves. ~Psalms 127:2

Then he said to them, "The Sabbath was made for man, not man for the Sabbath. ~Mark 2:27

What are Three ways you can improve your bedtime routine to get a more peaceful night rest?

Mental Health Check-In

DATE _____

HOW ARE YOU FEELING TODAY? _____

HOW ARE YOU FEELING TODAY?

HOW CAN YOU IMPROVE YOUR MENTAL HEALTH?

WHAT HAVE BEEN YOUR THREE DOMINANT EMOTIONS THIS WEEK?
- ○ _____
- ○ _____
- ○ _____

WHAT DO YOU FEEL GOOD ABOUT RIGHT NOW?

THINGS THAT TRIGGERS NEGATIVE EMOTIONS
- ○ _____
- ○ _____
- ○ _____
- ○ _____

MY RANKING OF MY MENTAL HEALTH THIS WEEK

☆ ☆ ☆ ☆ ☆

BODY AFFIRMATIONS AND DECLARATIONS

My Soul Deserves Rest

PERSONAL NOTE

Stop worrying when you lay down to rest. Try white noise or calming soothing music to help ease your mind and prepare it for rest.

SCRIPTURE

In peace I will lie down and sleep, for you alone, LORD, make me dwell in safety. ~Psalms 4:8

What is your nightly routine?

Mental Health Check-In

DATE _____

HOW ARE YOU FEELING TODAY?

HOW ARE YOU FEELING TODAY?

HOW CAN YOU IMPROVE YOUR MENTAL HEALTH?

WHAT HAVE BEEN YOUR THREE DOMINANT EMOTIONS THIS WEEK?
- _____
- _____
- _____

WHAT DO YOU FEEL GOOD ABOUT RIGHT NOW?

THINGS THAT TRIGGERS NEGATIVE EMOTIONS
- _____
- _____
- _____
- _____

MY RANKING OF MY MENTAL HEALTH THIS WEEK
☆ ☆ ☆ ☆ ☆

BODY AFFIRMATIONS AND DECLARATIONS

I Welcome the Healing Power of Christ into My Life. God Desires to Make Me Whole.

PERSONAL NOTE

Don't block God from healing you. Healing comes in many forms. Don't place limits on God.

SCRIPTURE

May God himself, the God who makes everything holy and whole, make you holy and whole, put you together - spirit, soul, and body - and keep you fit for the coming of our Master, Jesus Christ. The One who called you is completely dependable. If he said it, he'll do it! Friends, keep up your prayers for us. Greet all the Christians there with a holy embrace. And make sure this letter gets read to all the brothers and sisters. Don't leave anyone out. The amazing grace of Jesus Christ be with you!

Write Jesus a letter asking him to heal the different areas of your life.

Mental Health Check-In

DATE _____

HOW ARE YOU FEELING TODAY?

HOW ARE YOU FEELING TODAY?

HOW CAN YOU IMPROVE YOUR MENTAL HEALTH?

WHAT HAVE BEEN YOUR THREE DOMINANT EMOTIONS THIS WEEK?
- _____
- _____
- _____

WHAT DO YOU FEEL GOOD ABOUT RIGHT NOW?

THINGS THAT TRIGGERS NEGATIVE EMOTIONS
- _____
- _____
- _____
- _____

MY RANKING OF MY MENTAL HEALTH THIS WEEK
☆ ☆ ☆ ☆ ☆

MIND AFFIRMATIONS AND DECLARATIONS
SPIRITUAL AND EMOTIONAL HEALING

Bring your Thoughts & Concerns to God

PERSONAL NOTE

Anxiety will not take my mind away from what God called me to do on the earth. Getting your thoughts in alignment with what God says about you life will bring you closer to him on your walk of salvation. Knowing God is not punishing you but using this opportunity to intensivify your worship experience with him. God will reveal

SCRIPTURE

Do not be anxious about anything, but in every situation, by prayer and petition, with thanksgiving, present your requests to God. And the peace of God, which transcends all understanding, will guard your hearts and your minds in Christ Jesus. ~Philippians 4:6-7

Have you considered therapy or talking to a counselor about the impact health journey?

Mental Health Check-In

DATE _____

HOW ARE YOU FEELING TODAY? _____

HOW ARE YOU FEELING TODAY?

HOW CAN YOU IMPROVE YOUR MENTAL HEALTH? _____

WHAT HAVE BEEN YOUR THREE DOMINANT EMOTIONS THIS WEEK?
- _____
- _____
- _____

WHAT DO YOU FEEL GOOD ABOUT RIGHT NOW? _____

THINGS THAT TRIGGERS NEGATIVE EMOTIONS
- _____
- _____
- _____
- _____

MY RANKING OF MY MENTAL HEALTH THIS WEEK

☆ ☆ ☆ ☆ ☆

MIND AFFIRMATIONS AND DECLARATIONS
SPIRITUAL AND EMOTIONAL HEALING

Panic Attacks will NOT Have Dominion Over Me.

PERSONAL NOTE

God will guide you to the right doctor. If you are not getting fair treatment from your current physician take the

SCRIPTURE

The Lord replied, "My Presence will go with you, and I will give you rest." Exodus 33:14

How can your care team improve to better serve patients like you?

Mental Health Check-In

DATE _____

HOW ARE YOU FEELING TODAY?

HOW ARE YOU FEELING TODAY?

HOW CAN YOU IMPROVE YOUR MENTAL HEALTH?

WHAT HAVE BEEN YOUR THREE DOMINANT EMOTIONS THIS WEEK?
- _____
- _____
- _____

WHAT DO YOU FEEL GOOD ABOUT RIGHT NOW?

THINGS THAT TRIGGERS NEGATIVE EMOTIONS
- _____
- _____
- _____
- _____

MY RANKING OF MY MENTAL HEALTH THIS WEEK

☆ ☆ ☆ ☆ ☆

MIND AFFIRMATIONS AND DECLARATIONS
SPIRITUAL AND EMOTIONAL HEALING

I Will Live Peace

PERSONAL NOTE

Peace is obtainable. Often time's in the life of someone suffering with illness living a life full of peace seems impossible. Chronic illness and terminal illnesses require a as much if not more time than a full time job. There is no time off from illnesses. Which is why it is important to intentionally create a atmosphere that promotes sight sounds and scents that represent peace and promote wellness. An inexpensive idea is to hang eucalyptus in the shower. Benefits of eucalyptus in the shower. Stress reduction. For some people, the scent of eucalyptus can produce an immediate sense of calm. ...
Pain relief. ...
Respiratory health. ...
Sinusitis.

SCRIPTURE

LORD, be gracious to us; we long for you. Be our strength every morning, our salvation in time of distress." ~ Isaiah 33:2

What can you do to create a atmosphere of peace?

Mental Health Check-In

DATE _____

HOW ARE YOU FEELING TODAY? _____

HOW ARE YOU FEELING TODAY? _____

HOW CAN YOU IMPROVE YOUR MENTAL HEALTH? _____

WHAT HAVE BEEN YOUR THREE DOMINANT EMOTIONS THIS WEEK?

- _____
- _____
- _____

WHAT DO YOU FEEL GOOD ABOUT RIGHT NOW? _____

THINGS THAT TRIGGERS NEGATIVE EMOTIONS

- _____
- _____
- _____
- _____

MY RANKING OF MY MENTAL HEALTH THIS WEEK

☆ ☆ ☆ ☆ ☆

MIND AFFIRMATIONS AND DECLARATIONS SPIRITUAL AND EMOTIONAL HEALING

A Challenge will NOT Stop Me from Being Courageous

PERSONAL NOTE

God is with you through the whole process. God is our Shepard. As his sheep go through the hills and valleys of life God guides us with his voice. His voice speaks from a place we are heading towards. God in his infinite wisdom and ability to be Omnipresent navigates us through things we don't understand. God created doctors nurses and the health care system so he knows how to guide you through it with success.

SCRIPTURE

Have I not commanded you? Be strong and courageous. Do not be afraid; do not be discouraged, for the LORD your God will be with you wherever you go." ~ Joshua 1:9

Describe an experience you had to be courageous.

Mental Health Check-In

DATE _____

HOW ARE YOU FEELING TODAY?

HOW ARE YOU FEELING TODAY?

HOW CAN YOU IMPROVE YOUR MENTAL HEALTH?

WHAT HAVE BEEN YOUR THREE DOMINANT EMOTIONS THIS WEEK?
- _____
- _____
- _____

WHAT DO YOU FEEL GOOD ABOUT RIGHT NOW?
_____

THINGS THAT TRIGGERS NEGATIVE EMOTIONS
- _____
- _____
- _____
- _____

MY RANKING OF MY MENTAL HEALTH THIS WEEK
☆ ☆ ☆ ☆ ☆

FINANCES

God is My Source.

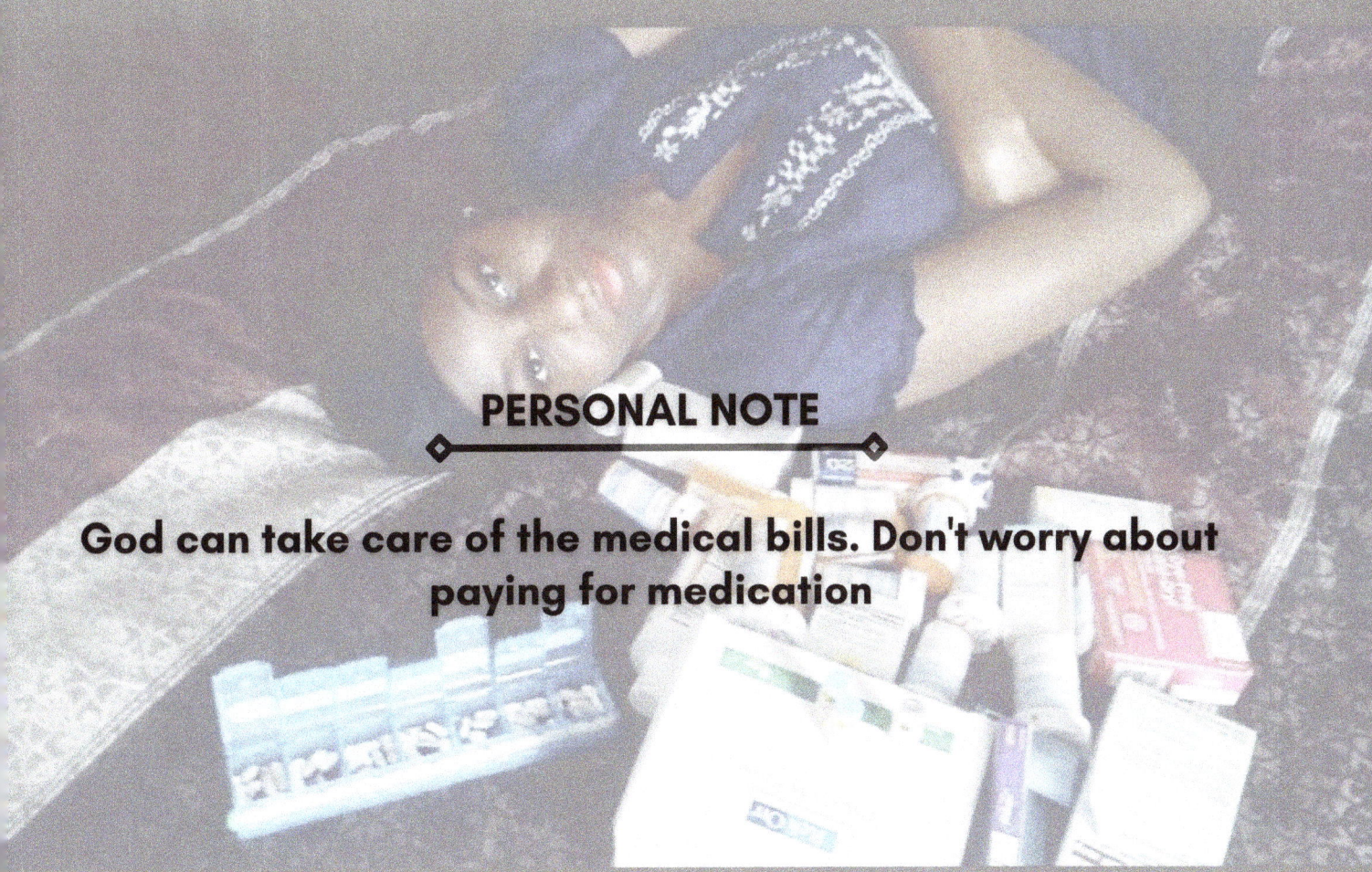

PERSONAL NOTE

God can take care of the medical bills. Don't worry about paying for medication

SCRIPTURE

The LORD is my shepherd, I lack nothing. ~Psalms 23:1

What do you need God to provide?

Mental Health Check-In

DATE _____

HOW ARE YOU FEELING TODAY? _____

HOW ARE YOU FEELING TODAY? _____

HOW CAN YOU IMPROVE YOUR MENTAL HEALTH? _____

WHAT HAVE BEEN YOUR THREE DOMINANT EMOTIONS THIS WEEK?
- _____
- _____
- _____

WHAT DO YOU FEEL GOOD ABOUT RIGHT NOW? _____

THINGS THAT TRIGGERS NEGATIVE EMOTIONS
- _____
- _____
- _____
- _____

MY RANKING OF MY MENTAL HEALTH THIS WEEK
☆ ☆ ☆ ☆ ☆

FINANCES

He is Sending Resources

PERSONAL NOTE

God will use your care team to advocate for you on your behalf.

SCRIPTURE

Surely your goodness and love will follow me all the days of my life, and I will dwell in the house of the LORD forever. ~Psalms 23:6

If money wasn't a issue what are 5 things you need right now?

Mental Health Check-In

DATE _____

HOW ARE YOU FEELING TODAY? _____

HOW ARE YOU FEELING TODAY? _____

HOW CAN YOU IMPROVE YOUR MENTAL HEALTH? _____

WHAT HAVE BEEN YOUR THREE DOMINANT EMOTIONS THIS WEEK?
- _____
- _____
- _____

WHAT DO YOU FEEL GOOD ABOUT RIGHT NOW? _____

THINGS THAT TRIGGERS NEGATIVE EMOTIONS
- _____
- _____
- _____
- _____

MY RANKING OF MY MENTAL HEALTH THIS WEEK

☆ ☆ ☆ ☆ ☆

FINANCES

I Lack Nothing

PERSONAL NOTE

Think Healthy. Think Big. Before God formed you he knew the type of life you would live. He knew the lifestyle you can handle. It is not God's will that we doubt his ability to take care of us.

SCRIPTURE

Nevertheless, I will bring health and healing to it; I will heal my people and will let them enjoy abundant peace and security."
~ Jeremiah 33:6

What does wellness mean to you in this stage of your life?

Mental Health Check-In

DATE _____

HOW ARE YOU FEELING TODAY? _____

HOW ARE YOU FEELING TODAY? _____

HOW CAN YOU IMPROVE YOUR MENTAL HEALTH? _____

WHAT HAVE BEEN YOUR THREE DOMINANT EMOTIONS THIS WEEK?
- _____
- _____
- _____

WHAT DO YOU FEEL GOOD ABOUT RIGHT NOW? _____

THINGS THAT TRIGGERS NEGATIVE EMOTIONS
- _____
- _____
- _____
- _____

MY RANKING OF MY MENTAL HEALTH THIS WEEK

☆ ☆ ☆ ☆ ☆

FINANCES

Whatever I Need is Paid in Full.

PERSONAL NOTE

A year into landing what I thought was my dream job working in a transitional home for women in recovery for substance . My illness progressed to the point I couldn't perform my job duties. Leaving a job under any circumstances can be devastating. Leaving a job because you suddenly became disabled can leave you in financial limbo. Talk to your doctor's and care team about what resources are able to help financially.

SCRIPTURE

"Say to those with fearful hearts, "Be strong, do not fear; your God will come, he will come with vengeance; with divine retribution he will come to save you."~Isaiah 35:4

Have you talk to anyone about how to pay down medical bills and expenses?

Mental Health Check-In

DATE _____

HOW ARE YOU FEELING TODAY? _____

HOW ARE YOU FEELING TODAY?

HOW CAN YOU IMPROVE YOUR MENTAL HEALTH? _____

WHAT HAVE BEEN YOUR THREE DOMINANT EMOTIONS THIS WEEK?
- _____
- _____
- _____

WHAT DO YOU FEEL GOOD ABOUT RIGHT NOW? _____

THINGS THAT TRIGGERS NEGATIVE EMOTIONS
- _____
- _____
- _____
- _____

MY RANKING OF MY MENTAL HEALTH THIS WEEK

☆ ☆ ☆ ☆ ☆

JOURNAL PAGES

About Diandra Williams

Diandra Williams was born in Providence, Rhode Island, on December 2, 1979. She is a mother of 4 children. Diandra was called to ministry at the age of 25 years old and became an elder of the church at 30 years. She has been serving the people for 17 years.

In 2012, Diandra was diagnosed with Rheumatoid Arthritis and Dermatomyositis. During the first year of her diagnosis, she looked on social media for life stories like hers. Without success, Diandra knew she had to share her health journey with people going through a sudden onset of chronic illness.

Diandra Williams understands that living with chronic illness is complicated, and no one should navigate it alone. "Matters of Healing: The Breaking Point," "Diandra Williams: Matters of Healing" affirmation and journal, and writing journal was created to be a beacon of light for someone looking for a sign of hope.

Matters of Healing

Get all 3 copies of Diandra Williams' "Matters of Healing" books.

"Matters of Healing: The Breaking Point" is the unedited raw thoughts written in real-time by Diandra Williams.

Every page was written from the heart of the author. She takes you on a mental and emotional rollercoaster by tackling various life issues, including but not limited to managing life with chronic illnesses, marriage, and ministry.

Living with a chronic illness is disruptive and unpredictable as it takes over a person's body, eventually affecting every area of your life.

"Diandra Williams: Matters of Healing Affirmation and Journal" walks the reader through her life's journey, starting with childhood and marriage, then ministry. In addition, the book talks about how medicine collided with everyday life when she was diagnosed with Rheumatoid Arthritis and Dermatomyositis. This diagnosis forever changed Diandra's life and propelled her to her true calling from God.

The journal is 50 page-lined paper book that allows users to write their thoughts.

Books are available on Amazon.

www.ingramcontent.com/pod-product-compliance
Lightning Source LLC
LaVergne TN
LVHW070532070526
838199LV00075B/6766